BABY BLUES® SCRAPBOOK NO. 5

We Are Experiencing Parental Difficulties... Please Stand By

Other Baby Blues Scrapbooks from Andrews and McMeel

BABY BLUES® SCRAPBOOK NO. 5

We Are Experiencing Parental Difficulties... Please Stand By

BY JERRY SCOTT AND RICK KIRKMAN

Andrews and McMeel
A Universal Press Syndicate Company
Kansas City

ISBN: 0-8362-1779-9

Library of Congress Catalog Card Number: 94-79702

98 99 00 01 02 BAH 10 9 8 7 6 5 4

10

BABY BLUES®

RICK KIRKMAN / BY JERRY SCOTT

I THINK I CAN HELP YOU GET ORGANIZED, WANDA.

DRAW A LINE DOWN THE CENTER OF THE PAPER. ON THE LEFT SIDE, WRITE ALL OF THE THINGS YOU NEED TO DO THAT ARE URGENT. ON THE RIGHT— ALL THE THINGS THAT CAN WAIT.

OKAY... I'LL TRY.

DONE?

MORE LIKE DONE-FOR.

KIRKMAN & SCOTT

SEE, ZOE? MOMMY MADE A LIST OF EVERYTHING SHE HAS TO DO TODAY.

IF I FOLLOW THIS LIST, I'LL BE PERFECTLY ORGANIZED, AND—

OH, NO! NOT THE PLANT AGAIN!

CRASH!

I SHOULD BE CLEANING UP THE KITCHEN NOW... WAIT-ZOE! DON'T THROW TOYS AROUND! STAY AWAY FROM THAT! AAAGH! NOT THE WALLS!

IF YOU LOVED YOUR MOMMY, YOU'D MESS UP SOMETHING THAT'S ON THE LIST!

KIRKMAN & SCOTT

NO, ZOE... THESE ARE MOMMY'S PAPERS. YOUR THINGS ARE OVER THERE.

LOOK AT THE PRETTY BLOCKS.

I LOVE THESE THINGS.

KIRKMAN & SCOTT

THEY'RE SO COLORFUL AND CHUNKY... I NEVER HAD BLOCKS THIS NICE WHEN I WAS A KID!

NO **WONDER** OUR CHECKBOOK NEVER BALANCES...

EEEKNGNUM ANGYUMEEBEE!

BABY BLUES®

RICK KIRKMAN / JERRY SCOTT

BEEP! BEEP!

MOM? WHEN I WAS A BABY AND IT WAS TIME FOR YOU TO CLEAN THE KITCHEN...

...DID YOU START WITH THE FLOOR OR THE CEILING?

BOY AM I BEAT! I WAS ON THE PHONE ALL DAY!

A LOT OF THEM WERE LONG DISTANCE! AREA CODE AND EVERYTHING! DID I MENTION THAT?

CAR PAYMENT... INSURANCE... MORTGAGE...

...CREDIT CARDS... UTILITIES...GROCERIES... TAXES... COLLEGE FUND FOR ZOE...

PENNY FOR YOUR THOUGHTS.

CASH?

25

26

BABY BLUES®

RICK KIRKMAN BY JERRY SCOTT

BABY BLUES®

RICK KIRKMAN / BY JERRY SCOTT

RING! RING!

WAAAAA!

HI, YOU'VE REACHED WANDA, MOTHER-AT-HOME...

...IF YOU CALLED TO SELL ME SOMETHING, PRESS ONE. IF YOU CALLED TO CHAT, PRESS TWO. IF YOU CALLED JUST TO WAKE UP THE BABY, PRESS THREE...

IF YOU WISH TO SPEAK TO A COHERENT PERSON, PLEASE CALL BACK SOME OTHER TIME.

ANOTHER ONE OF THOSE DAYS, HUH?

YOU SHOULD HAVE SEEN WHAT ZOE DID TODAY... IT WAS **SO** CUTE!

SHE GRABBED THAT PICTURE OF YOU THAT SITS ON THE BED-SIDE TABLE, AND SAID, "**DA-DA!**", AND STARTED KISSING IT.

AWWWW!

I'M GOING TO QUIT MY JOB.

WELL, OKAY, ZOE. JUST THIS ONCE...

WANDA!

WHAT??

LOOK AT YOURSELF! ONE MINUTE YOU'RE COMPLAINING THAT ZOE WON'T EAT HER OWN FOOD, AND THE NEXT MINUTE YOU'RE FEEDING HER OFF <u>YOUR</u> PLATE!

CHILDREN NEED CONSISTENCY! HOW IS SHE GOING TO LEARN ANYTHING IF WE'RE NOT CONSISTENT?

WE'RE CONSISTENT ABOUT INCONSISTENCY.

BABY BLUES

By Rick Kirkman / Jerry Scott

BABY BLUES®

BY RICK KIRKMAN / JERRY SCOTT

OBJECTS IN MIRROR ARE LOUDER THAN THEY APPEAR

47

Panel 1: SIXTY DOLLARS FOR A BOTTLE OF ANTIBIOTICS FOR ZOE! SIXTY BUCKS!

Panel 2: HAVE YOU EVER HEARD OF ANYTHING SO OUTRAGEOUS?

Panel 3: $40.00 BABY SHOES... $150.00 STROLLER... $10.00 BOX OF DIAPERS...

THAT WAS A RHETORICAL QUESTION.

UH-OH.

ZING! CLIP! TOINK!

WAAAA

ZING! CLIP! THAK!

Panel 1: WE JUST RAN INTO YOLANDA AND MIKE AT THE DRUGSTORE.

Panel 2: SHE'S EIGHT AND A HALF MONTHS PREGNANT. WHEW! REMEMBER THAT?

DO I EVER!

Panel 3: SWOLLEN FEET... UNCOMFORTABLE ALL THE TIME...

DIFFICULTY BREATHING... CRANKINESS...

Panel 4: POOR YOLANDA.

POOR MIKE.

57

BABY BLUES

RICK KIRKMAN / JERRY SCOTT

BABY BLUES®

RICK KIRKMAN / BY JERRY SCOTT

HEY, WANDA...

AWWWWW... LOOK AT THAT FACE.

SO YOUNG...

PHOTOS

SO FRESH...

PHOTOS

SO INNOCENT...

WELL, SHE WAS JUST A FEW HOURS OLD...

I'M TALKING ABOUT ME.

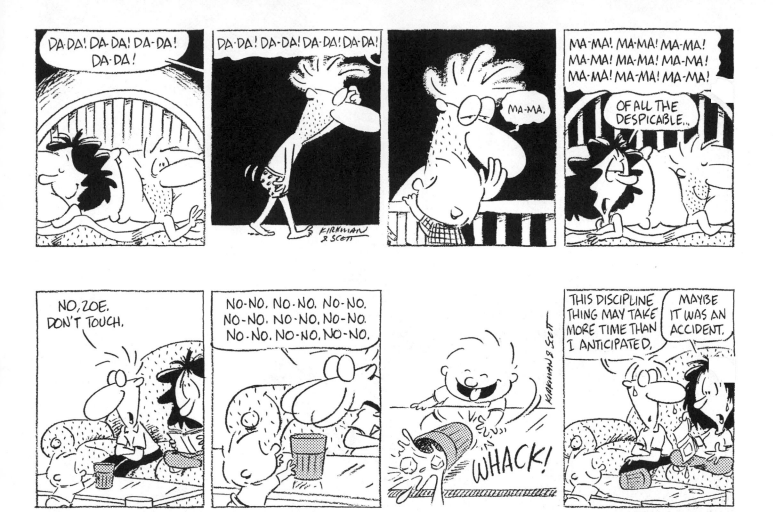

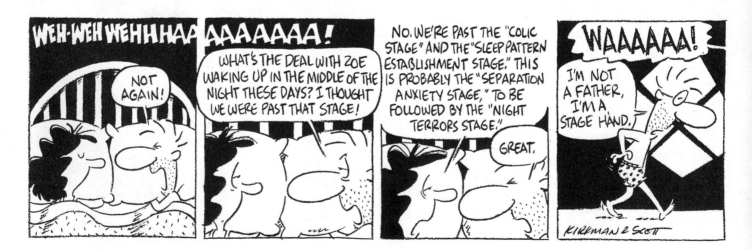

BABY BLUES®

BY RICK KIRKMAN / JERRY SCOTT

BEWARE OF BABY

YOU WANT YOUR BALL? OKAY, HERE'S YOUR BALL.
BA

WOW! ZOE IS PICKING UP WORDS ALREADY!

OH, YEAH, SHE CAN'T SAY TOO MANY YET, BUT SHE UNDERSTANDS A BUNCH... WATCH THIS.

ZOE, SHOW DADDY WHERE MIKE'S NOSE IS. WHERE'S MIKE'S NOSE?

RIGHT!
DOAT
WONK!

NOW, WHERE'S MIKE'S EAR?
DEAH!

YES! THAT'S MIKE'S EAR. WHERE'S MIKE'S CHIN?
DIN!
THWAK!

EYES. WHERE ARE MIKE'S EYES?

THAT'S ENOUGH! THAT'S ENOUGH! I BELIEVE YOU! CALL HER OFF!

DARRYL, MAYBE YOU SHOULDN'T SHOW OFF ZOE'S VOCABULARY ANY MORE THIS AFTERNOON.

WHY? DO YOU THINK SHE LOOKS TIRED?

BABY BLUES

BY RICK KIRKMAN / JERRY SCOTT

Hi, Honey. How was your day? **Fine.**

Any mail? **A couple of bills and some articles my mom clipped out for us.**

Articles? **Yeah. Stuff that she thinks we might find HELPFUL.**

Now, Wanda, I know that you think your mom is trying to tell us something, but, hey—it's no big deal.

I mean, we can't let a couple of magazine articles on mothering tips get under our skin.

Those are mine.

Yours are over there.

HEY!

OKAY, WE NEED TO GET ORGANIZED... HOW MUCH OF THIS STUFF DO WE NEED TO TAKE WITH US TO MOM & DAD'S?

OKAY. HOW MUCH OF THIS STUFF **DON'T** WE NEED TO TAKE WITH US TO MOM & DAD'S?

THE CARPETING... WE CAN LEAVE THAT.

WHAT'S WRONG WITH ZOE?

I THINK SHE MAY BE TEETHING AGAIN... IT'S ABOUT TIME FOR HER FIRST MOLARS.

WEH WEH WEH

BUT WE'RE GOING ON VACATION IN A COUPLE OF DAYS, YOU DON'T THINK THERE'S A CHANCE SHE'LL STILL BE TEETHING DURING THE CAR TRIP, DO YOU?

The sarcastic response in this panel has been judged too graphic for general audiences or the unmarried.

OH.

WEH! WEH! WEH!

I CAN'T BELIEVE IT! WE'RE LEAVING ON A 1200-MILE CAR TRIP IN A COUPLE OF DAYS, AND ZOE STARTS TEETHING AGAIN!

YOU KNOW WHAT WE HAVE TO LOOK FORWARD TO, DON'T YOU?

1200 MILES OF WHINING, WHIMPERING, AND WAILING.

RIGHT!

PLUS, ZOE MIGHT BE A LITTLE FUSSY, TOO.

VERY FUNNY!

84

85

HEY, NICE JOB! SHE NEVER SAW IT COMING.

IN FACE-WASHING, AS IN WAR, THE ELEMENT OF SURPRISE IS CRUCIAL.

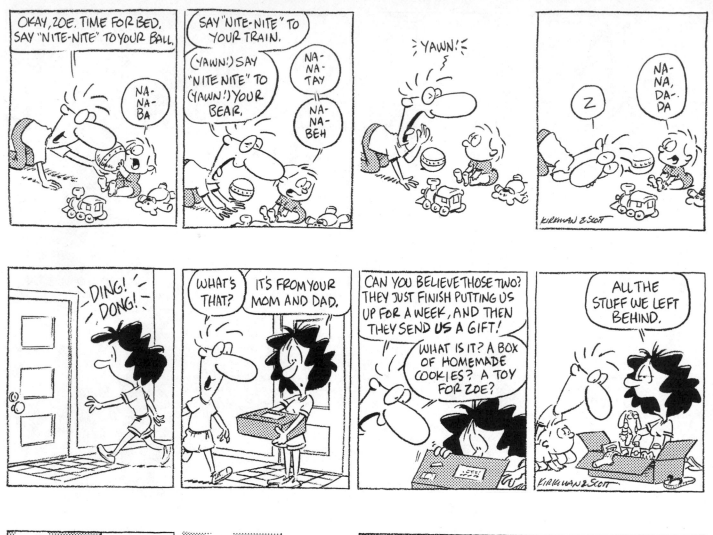

BABY BLUES®

RICK KIRKMAN / BY JERRY SCOTT

...AND THEN THE **HUGE** FU2ZY BEAR SWAM ACROSS THE **WIDE** RIVER TO WARN MISTER **KANGAROO!**

SHE'S ALMOST ASLEEP... MAYBE YOU SHOULD FINISH THE STORY TOMORROW NIGHT.

GOOD IDEA. I WANTED TO READ THE PAPER ANYWAY.

KIRKMAN & SCOTT

ECONOMIC **EXPERTS** REPORTED TODAY THAT THE **DEFICIT** ESTIMATES HAVE BEEN →MINIMIZED← BY Congress....

BABY BLUES®

BY RICK KIRKMAN / JERRY SCOTT

...AND AFTER CINDY AND I STOPPED OFF TO PICK UP OUR PULITZER PRIZES, WE WERE ABDUCTED BY ALIENS WHO MADE US THEIR KING AND QUEEN.

IT'S TRUE, EVERY WORD.

UH-HUH. THAT'S GREAT.

I THINK ZOE WAS BIGGER AT THAT AGE...I WONDER WHAT SHE'S DOING RIGHT NOW?

REALLY? HOW INTERESTING.

WHAT A CUTIE! HIS EYES ARE SO BIG! I WISH I COULD HOLD HIM.

THE TROUBLE WITH DINING OUT WITH NEW PARENTS

105

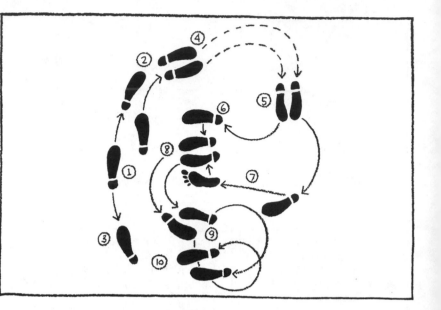

Panel 1: IT'S WEIRD STANDING HERE WATCHING ZOE SLEEP SO PEACEFULLY.

Panel 2: YOU'D NEVER GUESS THAT JUST AN HOUR AGO SHE WAS WREAKING HAVOC ON EVERYTHING WITHIN HER REACH.

YEAH... OR THAT ANY MINUTE SHE COULD WAKE UP AND DO IT ALL AGAIN.

Panel 3: KIRKMAN & SCOTT

Panel 4: IT'S SORT OF LIKE HAVING OUR OWN LITTLE MOUNT ST. HELENS IN A CRIB.

Panel 5: ...SMOOTH, RICH FLAVOR... HUSBAND TOLD ME THAT IF I SERVE THIS SALAD DRESSING AGAIN... MAXIMUM PROTECTION FOR THAT FRESH FEELING ALL... ♪ YEAH! YEAH! ♪ UH-HUH! WELL... HIGH 40s IN THE OUTLYING AREAS WITH OCCASIONAL SHOWERS...

KIRKMAN & SCOTT

Panel 6: I WISH YOU WOULDN'T LET ZOE CHEW ON THE REMOTE CONTROL.

IT'S JUST UNTIL HER TEETHING RING GETS COLD.

Panel 7: I LOVE SATURDAYS.

Panel 8: I FEEL LIKE JUST PUTTERING AROUND THE HOUSE DOING LITTLE REPAIR JOBS... WHAT DO YOU WANT ME TO FIX FIRST?

GEE, I DON'T KNOW...

Panel 9: WOULD YOU RATHER FIX THE STUFF THAT YOU BROKE WHILE YOU WERE TRYING TO FIX THE STUFF THAT NEVER GOT FIXED, OR JUST START ON THE STUFF YOU HAVEN'T ALREADY TRIED TO FIX TO BUILD UP YOUR CONFIDENCE?

KIRKMAN & SCOTT

Panel 10: ON SECOND THOUGHT, LET'S GO RENT A MOVIE.

114

BABY BLUES®

BY RICK KIRKMAN / JERRY SCOTT

Panel 1: OKAY, YOU TWO—HAVE FUN! / DON'T WORRY, WE HAVE EVERYTHING UNDER CONTROL. / ISN'T THIS GREAT?

Panel 2: IT WAS REALLY SWEET OF THEM TO WATCH THE KIDS THIS AFTERNOON SO WE CAN RELAX. / A WHOLE AFTERNOON FREE AND WE WON'T EVEN **TALK** ABOUT BABIES FOR A CHANGE!

Panel 3: "CHANGE"...THAT REMINDS ME—HOW MANY TIMES A DAY DID YOU CHANGE ZOE WHEN SHE WAS KEESHA'S AGE? / WE'RE NOT SUPPOSED TO BE TALKING ABOUT BABIES, BUT I THINK IT WAS ABOUT TEN.

Panel 4: GOOD, THAT'S ABOUT WHERE WE'RE AT... BUT LET'S CHANGE THE SUBJECT. / I THINK IT'S BECAUSE THEY EAT **ALL** THE TIME.

Panel 5: YOU GOT **THAT** RIGHT. I FEEL MORE LIKE A "MAMMARY" THAN A "MOMMY" THESE DAYS. / OH, THAT'LL CHANGE EVENTUALLY. WHAT ABOUT SLEEP?

Panel 6: I'D SAY FOUR HOURS AT A TIME. DID I TELL YOU WHAT KEESHA DID THE OTHER NIGHT WHEN— / OH! THAT REMINDS ME! WHEN ZOE WAS JUST A MONTH OLD WE USED TO ALWAYS...

Panel 8: CUT IT OUT, WE'RE SUPPOSED TO BE OUT HERE **NOT** TALKING ABOUT BABIES, REMEMBER? / YOU DIDN'T **NOT** TALK ABOUT YOURS FIRST!

120

121

123

127

The End